Incendiary Forefronts
and
Other Commotions

Other books of poetry by Thomas Walker:

Ashes In My Skull

Book III......Conundrum En Passant

Incendiary Forefronts
and
Other Commotions

poems by

Thomas Walker

Thomas Walker Publications

Eagle River, Alaska

For Information:

Thomas Walker Publications
26010 White Spruce Drive
Eagle River, Alaska 99577
www.thomas-walker-institute.com
Email: contact@thomas-walker-institute.com

Library of Congress Control Number: 2014911065
ISBN 978-0692240236
First Edition

1 3 5 7 9 10 8 6 4 2

To
all of my typewriters.

The warm breeze finds us lying down.
Incendiary thoughts behind the clown,
laughing at the light inside the house of strange.

I think that something is following me.
I hear it, I feel it, I see it......more frequently.
Eyes, black as the death of deep dark space;
the place of rest for poets and martyrs.

Contents

Lady Bane 1

He was just Here a moment ago 2

Monster of Malice 3

He Said, She Said 4

Hello, Goodbye 6

The Garter Snake 7

Angel Overboard 10

By the By(e) 11

Intensity 12

Pernicious Beauty 14

Pass Me the Binoculars 16

Right Behind 18

Whatever it Takes 19

Another Glimpse 20

Kill the King 21

Nostrum Agony 22

The Hauteur Hawk 23

Machete Lupine 24

Palace of Retreat 25

Now Will Never Come Again 26

Palace of a Legend 28

Glass Satire 29

Silent as Mist 30

Squandering 31

Death Conspires a Bestial Manifest 32

Every Grain 34

Archeologist of the Mind 35

Sedulous Instant in some Tolstoy-like Dream 36

Each Passing Year 38

Damn Nymphs 40

Surety 42

Stains 43

The Narrows 44

Dear Mr. Mouse, ...46

No Matter Who You Kill, Life Will Always Be Around 47

Comet of Love 50

Keep the Change 51

Watching You 52

Farewell 53

Dark Horse 54

86 Billion Neurons Why 56

The Keys Don't Tap the Same Anymore 58

Seagull Girl 60

Wheeled and Dealed 62

If I Find My Girl 64

Butterfly Servants 65

The Tale of Johnny Ice 68

Think No. 236369 69

The First Star I See 70

Angel Scream 72

Truth's Yield 73

Spotlight Love 74

Painted Desert 75

Over Your Shoulder 76

Poetic Slur 78

Confused Lady 79

Shadows Under the Rainbow 80

My Senses are Being Stripped 82

From a Poet's Vantage Point 83

Designed Fate 84

Who is the Artist 85

The Gondolier 86

Another Day 88

The Stainless Steel Vault 89

Wet 90

Miss America 91

Oracle of the Cephalopod 92

Leeway 94

Hell's Hundred Hectares 95

The Temptuous Temptress Empress 96

The Kangaroo 98

Misery Loves Calligraphy 99

Isms 100

Incendiary Forefronts
and
Other Commotions

Lady Bane

Lady Bane, the instigator
of hopeless lost love.
Her poetry engraved
on the walls of my mind.
My mind, the infinite
barrier of steel.
How heavy you feel.

How heavy I feel
with these visions of you
in the garden of blue
ever so vaguely aligned,
passionately side by side
in endless rows of two;
endless rows of you.

He was just Here a moment ago

I sit inside the golden hourglass
'neath the Tree of Ténéré.
People learn to forget but never to forgive;
learn to love but never to live.

We have had our fun
but now......the day is done.
Say goodbye to Mr. Sun;
the sand is sinking slowly.

She said, "It is strange
how you always seem to be
in your own little world;
you must be mad!"

I said, "It is the only place
where people know me
and do not care who I am;
is that so bad?"

Monster of Malice

Take a trip to the crystal palace
Take a drink from the immortal chalice,
and watch yourself change into a monster of malice.

Everybody's out looking for the strange and new.
Baby, don't you know it's oh so true,
because sometimes you're out there, looking too.

And out there, you begin to realize
that no one, no one, can criticize......
the way you hide behind your eyes.

Life is too short when love is strong,
if you have none, it seems too long,
and in the middle......everything feels wrong.

Eventually you will become numb and lose touch;
a nihilist, who will cease to care too much
about love, gods, angels, and such.

Because no one really cares if you die,
but if you know 'when', then they want to know 'why',
and if you don't......you better have an alibi.

No one could love me half as much as you,
but you couldn't love, the way I wanted you to.
So, you'll never know what it's like......to get on through.

He Said, She Said

You know, you know......it is no use;
life, always the same,
life, always deranged.
Why bother lying,
why bother trying
when all has been arranged?

Sure, sure......it is what it is;
but whatever can I do
to get on through to you.
It is amazing to me
how you couldn't see
that our love never grew.

I see, I see, short intervals of time
that you spent confused,
as we slowly diffused
in the hours of darkness,
and all of its starkness,
but you always refused.

I know, I know, very well
but care not to mention;
what exactly was your intention.
It all seemed so fast,
it never could last,
and you had no apprehension.

Yeah, Yeah, it is not very unlikely
that it was all my fault;
bringing our love to a halt.
For when I was in pain,
you prayed for more rain,
and filled my wounds full of salt.

I, I, must confirm
that I have overcome the fear
of not having you near.
For when I needed you most,
you were just like a ghost,
you would always disappear.

Hello, Goodbye

I fell for a girl
(once)
for a moment
or so;
ex-
changed a few
starry-eyed
glances,
thought of my
chances......
and said,
"I enjoyed
yours
(slowly)
as if there were
no tomorrow."
 (slowly)
I walked
a-
way
(withdrew),
and laughed
at the
(oozing)
mess
left behind.

The Garter Snake

Curveaceous woman
I am elongated, shining;
your presence enthralling,
your body immaculate.
Why can I not get inward
to the private fantasy
awaiting the happy?
To think of your love
enclosing about me......
I just can't take it anymore.
Can you hear me tapping
tapping at your door?

I just can't seem to find the time
to think about anything but being with you,
for an hour......or two.
Yes, it is true,
dissonance is improvement;
dressed up, ill-bred people
in a run around sort of way.
A hunting man and a debauched appetite;
head poised,
seeking a vow
to take into unfruitful corners.
A moderate excursion
delivering......
a fatal confinement.

I went into another room.
The faint voices of happy people,
the walls and the ceiling
were still......there.
I cannot rid of the domestic insects.
The generous beast
indicates his prey,

a new and polished woman.

Taking my lance
of wondrous length,
piercing my enemies
with unusual force;
arms at their sides
legs writhing,
'til down, down they fall.
Beloved loving,
the charlatan......can make you
(one solitary liquid).

Thrashing everywhere
is hopeless flesh.
Making promises in bed
that cannot be kept.
Midnight temple in the autumn
brings a breeze;
the poison in the snake
brings a goddess to her knees.

Her flower-soft breasts
needing to be caressed.
Oh perfumed child,
tell me your secrets.
I like what I see.
I see fury
in the reflections of your lips;
let me hold onto your hips.
My ship's mast is alive;
let me pull dockside
into your harbor.
No more games, no more tricks,
just liquid sanctity.

Sirens go off and hatred begins;
the surmise of love / for a while......
until lust comes lurking.

Nude elegance and wasted years.
Planting a rose garden;
moaning and moaning
over what you cannot have.

Obscure day dreams
lost in the honey factory.
A silent and shame faced recluse
smoking his thoughts away;
the unlikely tease of poetry.
the somber loneliness.
the composer of love is lost......
in the honey factory.

Disillusioned by criticism itself,
who is a worthy member of society?
Quarrel upon my speculations
standing erect, pulsating
in hues fit for everyone's body.
The ignorant reader will elaborate
on their anxiety.

Suddenly, an anonymous pair of thighs
appears in the daylight causing strife.
With the boldest lash of a whip
it all comes to an end.
The ravenous ecstasy
as an artificial moment thickens,
and is completed
with a reliable ooze.

Silence the snakes hiss,
give him a little kiss......
give him a little kiss......

Angel Overboard

You should have seen her
walk into the room.
The gems around her neck
symbolizing doom,
and the sumptuous glow
in her velvet-like eyes
pulling everyone in,
like a whirlpool in disguise.

Can you hear me?
Can you hear me?
Can you hear me,
angel overboard?

With movements
of ancient pageantry,
no one is so great
a delight to see.
Every element embedded
in the most recent memory,
inspiring hope
for the next century.

Let me talk to you.
Let me talk to you.
Let me talk to you,
in my sleep.

By the By(e)

I put my blues in a bottle,
sent them out to sea.
If anybody ever finds it,
they'll know where to find me.

I came down the other day
to watch it all go up in flame.
Back to the bell tower,
like the hunchback of Notre Dame.

I've got my blues in a bottle,
just waiting to explode.
I've got my heart in the freezer;
never to corrode.

Walking through the sun,
I have never felt so close to death.
I will love you all night long, babe,
if you just let me catch my breath.

There is no ship inside this bottle,
just grounded guts and blood;
floating along the shoreline,
and waiting for the flood.

Life has played you for the fool;
graduated from the school of paying dues.
You say you're looking for work,
you'd like a job singing the blues?

Many are applying for the position;
I am sorry, but you are overqualified.
If I could give you a bit of advice;
consider something in suicide.

Intensity

One day a monstrous
dark black cloud / smoky
overflow / signaled to me.

"I am Intensity,
you have freed me.
I give you virgins - 3 -,
yours / all yours,
labyrinthine intimacy
not to be mistaken for love."

Bountiful pleasures
can excel your hopes.
Prosper at night
only to see the daylight
come around once again.

……the smoke dissipates.

The saturnine poets appear;
misery's company must be near.
Common empires relax the mind;
rhythmic dreams caught from behind.
The lost, the forgotten, the meek, the sublime;
applauding death, 'the conqueror of time.'

Turbulent residuum ,
and a thoughtless commotion
caused by a seductive look;
by hook or by crook
the smoke has returned.

My engine is now stuck on number two,
it will not stop until it gets to you,
and makes you come……

come with me......
come with me......
come with me.
Hands around
the head of the snake.
Mine is yours,
yours to take.
Take me to
the infinite lake......
full of pearls.

Pernicious Beauty

Yesterday, I caught you gazing in the mirror,
you looked so hypnotized.
You never know what you're going to see;
me looking at you, you looking at me.

Pick a memory
and throw it aside.
How about one
that you've denied?

My fingers are going numb;
come here and let me touch your lips.
Spread out your dreams for me;
I'll cut them into little strips.

The summertime is so sweet,
everyone loves the heat,
until the sweat pours into their eyes.
And the headless horseman cries
while you laugh and say,
"It is not my problem."

Jaded memories, razor sharp and bleeding,
of the moment I gave you my token.
The tears arrive and I wonder how it all went by,
when not a word was spoken.
Leaving me stranded in a forgotten corridor;
the air is thin, I think I'm choking.
Now you say you feel like love,
I know you must be joking.
You can't, you don't know how,
and anyway, my heart is already broken.
My head feels like a dried out skull
that you would stumble upon
walking through desert sands.

I will never give you my heart,
you will never give me yours.
We will be another moment
passing through swinging doors.
I will wonder what went wrong,
you will wonder what went right.
We will always think about it,
in the darkest depths of night.

How riches turn to rags,
and rags turn to dust;
when hearts stop pounding,
and love turns back to lust.

We met on the road to nowhere,
we split up around the bend;
and if you're feeling lonely,
this message I will send:

Sometimes you know,
love can grow......
so co-ooo-old
you've got to build a fi-ire,
and let it burn......
let it burn......
let it burn, burn, burn.
Just let it burn.

The heat is pouring in,
and the end is about to begin.
My eyes are a two-way mirror,
image projections.
I see right through you,
you see only reflections.

Pass Me the Binoculars

Another valiant effort
by the Richter people,
but not good enough;
for Humankind's steeple
is built to last,
one lonely coward
says to the other.

Strong, soaring capitalistic needs;
feeds......the median populace.
So beguiled, with tiled
patterns on her doorstep;
who is Mother here......
computer science?

Dolorous dolphin, you are fine;
there is no reason to smile.
Just take another deep breath,
and go down under for a while.

Incantations repeated
for risqué ritual,
satisfy the baboon.
Take me to your forest
says Mr. Raccoon,
I'd sure like to take something
from those fucking baboons.
Maybe a Mercedes Benz,
or just some garbage.

Hey, Mr. Giraffe,
I know you see up high,
but can you see clear?
Bring your head down here.
See everybody drinking beer,

trying to be like what they see;
Living simple synchronicity.
You might get laid,
it is an aphrodisiac.
You can lift your head back,
up into a mushroom cloud.
You should be proud.

I think we better get out of here,
lickety-split,
One lonely coward
says to the other.
I'm afraid of you,
your afraid of me,
we may have started something
like World War Three.
Just you and me?
For heaven's sake,
that is all it would really take.

Right Behind

I'm sorry that I got hung up
in your railroad.
You see, it is usually
not like me,
fortunately.

To get stuck riding down
the Lonely Lover's Railway,
heading straight
for the bottom of the sea,
unfortunately.

It is something that the brakeman
learns to live with;
in this strangled up,
heartless society,
fortunately.

For you can never take away
his immortal friend,
who goes by the name,
'Lady Misery',
unfortunately.

She is always right behind
snickering.
Without these situations
my words could never be,
fortunately.

Whatever it Takes

Madonna seems so relentless in her pose;
stoical serenity from her head down to her toes.
She stands torn between facts and a wish;
compelled into accepting eternity on a dish.
Her head thrown back as though to scream;
give me access to contemplate in dream.
Apocalyptic messages for those who cannot see;
occasional glimpses through ordinary forms of poetry.

Mary reminding us of inadequate frontiers in hell;
prodigally presented, ever so well.
Brilliantly suggestive, but still just a guess;
we'll find out for ourselves, none the less.
Her idolatrous beauty there for all to take;
spread wide open, only for heaven's sake.
Do what you have to do, to get in there;
even if it means you have to walk on air.

Another Glimpse

I think I caught
another glimpse
of humanity;
death blossoms
to infinity.
What is this cadaver doing
right in front of me?
Is it a sign, sign/symbol
to be free?
No-no-no-no……
I am just fading away
through the floor;
think I'll wake up
on the Dead Sea shore.
Who is this woman coming,
must be a whore?
She said, I am here
to save your forgotten lore.
No-no-no-no……
get up now,
and let us go for a swim.
We don't have much time,
the lights are getting dim.
She said, Relax,
stop looking so grim.
You know we are
going to make love
on a whim.
No-no-no-no…...

Kill the King

Come inward with thee oppressed;
back outward with thee distressed.
Sign posts (universal), King Lear is everywhere;
listen and you will hear (the air).
Below me, may it be so delightful;
above me, may it be so frightful.
Over money, time, and bottles of wine we dwell;
beneath every institution lives a poet in hell.
Yet, ours is not to reason why;
ours is just to do or die.

Are you committed......
to humanity?
Are you committed......
to technology?
Or are you committed......
to beauty;
the wisdom of morality
(not the morality of wisdom)?

I cannot laugh, but I have once tried;
all of my faith has been denied.
Devoured by fire in the hollow dungeon of pain;
bludgeoning fools with nothing to gain.
You run, you run, you run, and you run;
all those afraid to stand in front of a gun.
So we give up hope, then in come the guards;
their presence seen all through the graveyards.
And forever we will march, and forever we will sing;
kill the king, kill the king, I should've killed the king.

Nostrum Agony

Come with me, in harmony,
share thee; nostrum agony.
Look in - to the sunlamp,
untimely evacuation from
what is real (feel it).
Orgiastic energies,
break - up of
existence,
play - out
the gamine.
Neptune's wives, the urchins;
call upon them.
The delectable but deadly
saboteurs of
common love.
Once again, I fall victim
to sultry Sara;
oh, the synergistic tendency.
Come with me in harmony.

The Hauteur Hawk

Mock on,
poet or prognosticator.
People now must see (eye to eye)
to believe
and believe (the eyes have it)
to see.

Because you do not understand,
the metaphor
is merely
the evening of life.
The evening of life (I see)
is a tumultuous thought.
Can you see it in my eyes?
Can you see the path
the hauteur hawk flies?

Quietly, the poet or prognosticator
swoops down upon the alley,
where the dreamers gather,
to conjure up a grand finale.

A vision of tomorrow;
a vision of the past.
A vision fading softly;
a vision fading fast.

The hawk flapped its wings
three times,
looked back,
and said:
"It is too bad I didn't turn out
to be everything you wanted
me to be."

Machete Lupine

Machete
lupine,
deceitful flower,
pierce your enemies
while they cower.
Enigmatic hopelessness,
concubine of power;
renascent love
soars by the hour.
End of love,
life to devour;
a wealth of misery
inside the glass tower.

Palace of Retreat

Eloquently,
in the back of his mind,
loathes a girl
in silky shiny clothes;
a doleful regression
of the soul.

Delphinium girl,
deliver the fatal blow.
Create a slaughter and
look at the effulgent
pose of the sun.
The price of her
super fire (deadly heat);
a palace of retreat.

Now Will Never Come Again

Conflict in the time between ages 18 and 65:
The religion of youth
is unlike that of old age.
Youths will strive for knowing,
the purpose of discovery.
Who is strong, who is weak,
who is bright, who is bleak,
who has the courage
to fight humankind's mystique?
They hope to go out with much
more than they arrived with.

In the dissimilar universe of old age,
success is defined, or perhaps
failure is accepted.
Either way the boundaries
have been touched,
and expectations laid to rest.
Living......is the quest.

Conflict in the time between ages 18 and 65:
Finding a reason to stay alive;
what is new......is sacred.
Behold the youth,
attaching themselves to the birth
of philosophies.

Closing in on death,
what is new......is evil.
The old answers of existence
have come with great pain.
Lock the door and go away,
for antiquity laughs at today
with great disdain.

Yet wrapped up inside......
is a belief,
a religion,
a spirit,
a philosophy,
a style.
Moreover, a feeling......
a feeling of conflict.
It is the emotion of conflict
that makes the man in this world.
Changes every day
present us with such conflict.
One may retreat
to the corner of the mind,
and ignite that feeling just the same.

Releasing our energy
we may take control of life
and today, concurrently.
But in the final scene,
fate will surrender
to the feeling of conflict.

Can you feel it aiming at your head?
You better run, before you are dead.

I consider myself a man
without name,
without category.
I do not know the poet.
I do not know the artist.
I do not know the architect.
I do not know the thinker.
I do not know the victor.
I only know......
a man of the moment.

Palace of a Legend

Take a drink
from the chalice of martyrdom,
'tis the palace of a legend.
Emergence of the individual
in the outcome of choice.
Emergence of the individual
in the opinions we voice.

And to this......
the green-eyed goddess answered.
Take another drink
from the chalice of martyrdom.
The ground is bloody;
awake from your unnatural sleep.
Sleep?
Sleep is impossible in this cavern.
I beg your pardon, sir?
It is my home, you know!

Sing for me, muse,
we have a long way to go.

And so comes the end
of another season,
as science turns against us.
Loch Ness......
does have a monster after all,
in the depths of this abyss.
The planet earth is blessed
with life,
and naturally
we are suspicious.

Glass Satire

I am a cactus in the rain.
Reign, protruding and spindly,
a cultivation of that which is art.
At what juncture
do you consider me sacred?
Not lineal enough for the median populace,
(collecting portions of chaos/poetry)
amongst them, Euphrates and followers.
Great numbers of followers
so shrewd in clock management.
A famous poet will call it by name,
"glass satire".
Rejoice that the empire is governed
by the imperial majesty and not Ivanhoe,
Ivanhoe the terrible.
Measurement of success occurs
long before death.
Golden blonde love toys
searching for success in their own way.
Mother of indulgence,
or just a plaything,
and gentlemen always show up
for the execution.
In our America
this pleasure boat is overflowing,
full of maids of honor.
An effervescent rush
which I have already described,
greedily devoured by Barbie.

Silent as Mist

Maybe it is thought?
I am mad that I killed
with no tears for my victims,
with no bereavement for my actions.
What crime is today?
Thou shall not kill?

Thou shall not understand worship.
Just another wounded lion
left behind to die in the heat.
Another American tragedy,
thinking too much.
There are undeniable differences
between a thinking man
and the rest.

Beware of vitality in a box.
A wild sanctuary
pent up with anger
......the birth of a nation.
The menacing world of civilization,
its rise or the fall,
is the warrior's call.

Squandering

I cannot quite
remember when.
I think I was
squandering
at the age of ten,
somewhere
in the mountains
of Pennsylvania.
But then......again,
I am not exactly sure
why I was there.
Yet somehow,
wandering
off on my own,
I witnessed
a world all alone.
Serenity was
all that I heard,
the fluttering wings
of a hummingbird.

Death Conspires a Bestial Manifest

Butterfly renaissance,
the damage is unbelievable.
Focal point of what is left,
a promising life somehow ends.
A brand new world
a prism sends
for those who dare.

Breathing smoke,
the warrior dragon
feeds the fires;
a bestial manifest
of death conspires.

What grand noise of storm and tempest.
Go forth into the holes of the rocks,
and into the caverns of the earth.
The wrathful suffrage of birth
is to grow, and to learn
that you will likewise perish.

I am saying to you,
that you alone can bring down
the glass tower,
with but one stone.
A simple costume makes a drone.
Defiant wretches of a new age
led blindly by their sage,
until utter ruin
and permanent destruction come.

Still conspiring,
are the smooth-sounding hordes of locusts.
Millions of false prophecies
piping dreams from their own trill.

Kill and kill,
two billion with one stone.
A simple costume makes a drone.

A survival technique
written in virtuosity,
says that somehow
we all just evolve differently.
Whoso uses the unknown sense,
the immense......glory?
There are no victories in life,
only in death.
Those who survive respond the best.
The rest......
just a representation
of the hopeless benign.
This is a world......
a world that could be divine.
Praise the immortal sign
of her hair,
rolling and flowing
across the breast.
Death conspires a bestial manifest.
Nothing but nothing
is invulnerable in nature.

Every Grain

My love is in every grain;
an hourglass full of pain.

In the crystalline whirlpool
I let go of your hand.

Watching you fall,
softly you land;
and in no time at all,
united we stand.

If you want to build castles,
there is plenty of sand.
Sometimes life
reverses as planned.

My love is in every grain.
Let us do it again,
and again,
and again.

Archeologist of the Mind

Have you ever stopped to think
......Freudian shingles,
fruits in the ocean,
hypnotic back pains,
grains of sunshine,
slipstream parachute to death,
or an appointment to coma?
Army ants marching in your sleep
......the ordered sleep,
trade winds in turmoil,
abnormal patterns in
the area of the brain
involving memory.
Unusual erotic explosions;
it is good of you to come with me.
Genetic evolution,
island universes
filtered in the eggshell
of humanity.
A cartoon atmosphere
in pursuing happiness;
run cheetah run and never stop
the day you do is the day you drop.
Cylinder pleasures,
he finds with pride;
oozing to watch
her notions glide.
Pandemonium breaks loose
in effervescent moon glow;
stand back and watch
the passion plasma flow.

Sedulous Instant in some Tolstoy-like Dream

Never underestimate
an underestimator.

Those who want to flee,
osculate the sun
as you meander through the daisies.
Those who stay hidden,
buried in the sand,
walking through the mazes.
Those who choose to live,
herded one by one,
brainwashed by the dailies.

Want to hear me sling
arrows of hatred at the brain?
Don't worry, 'tis not in disdain.
Come with me crawling my dear.
Winter is nonexistent this year,
but you are so cold,
and my heart's made of gold.
A story so common,
a story so old.

Come with me crawling my dear;
life is so filled
with drear......iness.
Have no fear;
the upcoming days
will be quiet and warm.
Come with me crawling my dear;
the poet's life is filled
with drear......iness.
Look at my watch and begin to scream;
I wish it was all just a dream.

Close your eyes
and you can still hear;
come with me crawling my dear.
Hatred has to give birth,
shortly after the mirth.
The windows in my heart
are cracking
from shear......stress.

Everybody says, god bless,
as they look up the dress
of a beautiful angel.
Such a precious moment,
the virgin Mary speaks
to America today.
Do you want to hear?
Come with me crawling my dear.
Follow me crawling my dear;
suicide dreams
in the clear......white sky.

You can just blink and hope,
looking down at the bottom
from the top
of the slope......of happiness.
Knowing that you're going to die,
ask yourself one last time......why
did I get cursed
so as to be here with you?

Each Passing Year

Ribbons and bows,
ribbons and bows;
everybody thinks they know
where the water flows.
But what do you know,
what do you know
about me.

The bend of a tree,
the crack of the moon;
everybody comes undone
by mid-afternoon.
But what do you see,
what do you see
about me.

Visions of right,
visions of wrong;
visions of sorrow
all day long.
But what do you feel,
what do you feel
about me.

Moments you seize,
moments let go;
what are you doing
after the show?
Would you like to be,
would you like to be
with me?

Driving rain,
whistling wind;
whatever it takes,

my heart is determined.
But what do you say,
what do you say
to me.

Feeling low,
feeling high;
feeling like
I want to die.
But how do you feel,
how do you feel
about me.

Into the ocean,
into the creek;
another idea lost
because I couldn't speak.
But what do you hear,
what do you hear
about me.

City at dusk,
city at dawn;
everybody in it
is just a pawn.
But what do you think,
what do you think
about me.

Almost there,
but I'm still here;
getting closer
with each passing year.
But do you shed a tear,
do you shed a tear
for me.

Damn Nymphs

My feelings remain submerged;
I will always be scarred now.
Part of me would like to rid of you.
Another, would like to know how.

Fighting from deep within
is the most important part;
the part that will forever debilitate,
the love that's in my heart.

The waves of her hair,
the way a nymph brings despair;
the way she wears her guile.

----

beginning - middle - end

She had an eagerness to escape,
until she crossed a poisonous snake;
stuck in hell for a while.

I am not a machine, programmed futility.
I am a human being, a category of hostility.
Ancillary beliefs fill the skull with snickering,
in patterns, like a television screen flickering.
Similarity is revered, as Orpheus holds his own.
Help me if I am falling, or else leave me alone.

It has been something less.
I must acquiesce;
a feeling as light as a feather.
Although I have been
to the underworld within,
I cannot explain this weather.

I will run with you slowly,
I will run with you wholly;
taking a trip to the moon.
Who knows girl,
you might find a pearl
along the way to Neptune.

Feel the softness of the rose,
with the thorn juxtaposed;
bleeding inside of the mind.
You will never realize
how blood flows from the eyes,
if you are not the hurting kind.

I have been higher than high,
then wanting to die;
a sorrow laden within.
Questions out of sync,
being pushed to the brink,
the joy of living in sin.

You see, you see, if you want to live with me;
you are going to have to love, passionately.
Because the story I tell is of a lover gone mad;
it might make you happy, it might make you sad.
That is the way it goes, in a ghosted town;
where up is only up, when you've just fallen down.

I have walked in the darkness of night
waiting for each day's light,
head shaking, taking a deep breath.
Another day is nearing,
another day of fearing
you are one day closer, closer to death.

Surety

I know that you don't really care,
but somehow you're always there.

Look at you,
look at me,
giving ourselves up
to prove that we are free.

The free,
free illusions,
expressing confusions;

one day she loves you,
the next day she leaves you.

Life is repetition,
morbid repetition;
nature's rendition
of going insane.

It is so hard to explain,
but I am leaving
in my own obscurity.
Of this, the surety
I will be back again,
but never
quite the same.

It is never
quite the same.

Stains

Inside the demons have control,
outside, they unfold my dreams.

Pay no attention to her thighs,
a heartless melody in the eyes.
The more you're with her,
the more you're hypnotized.

It takes darkness to feed her goals.
The outcome, in streams,
falling......falling......
falling to the floor.

Desperately, the broken angels
find their way back home.

Now you'll never forget me;
let go of your sanity,
welcome your misfortunes,
and welcome your destiny.

Don't forget to pick up all the pieces;
the lies you tell even the score.
The mess you make,
the mess you made,
leaves me with stains on the floor.

The Narrows

My body hurts all over
from the aches and the pains.
Oh, what would you think
if I blew out my brains?

I've been writing far too long
for love, torn, to arrive.
Oh, what would you think
if I took a great dive,
from the height, the peak,
the straight of the narrows;
the final refuge
for slings and arrows?
The last of sight,
the last of sound
beneath the waters,
a murky ground.

Such a high time to turn,
to walk away, and then to run.
Who wants to wait around,
staring into the sun?

And it just drives me crazy,
the downs and the downs
of everyday hell.
Most often protected,
hidden, so no one can tell
that deep inside you are dying.

Maybe someday, maybe someday,
in a far away land.
Maybe someday, right around here,
we'll wander through the mountains
and we'll disappear.

Right around here.
Right around here.

Is not life,
just a promise of ending,
to make you deny
all those pretending;
like society governing
all of your action,
then gone in the split
of a decimal fraction.

I do not know, I do not know,
how much longer I can take it.
What else is left
storming in the brew?
Life goes on,
with or without you.

Dear Mr. Mouse,

What are you going to do,
Mr. Mouse?
You have to
come out, come out,
come out of your house.
Sometimes it is time,
sometimes, Mr. Mouse.
Perhaps today,
perhaps right now;
you can head to the city
to feed the little kitty.

Get out of your house,
please, Mr. Mouse.
Everyone has to,
everyone must.
As time goes by,
I will gain your trust.
I know that I will,
sooner or later.
I hope, for your sake,
you are not an instigator.

Yours sincerely,
Cat

No Matter Who You Kill, Life Will Always Be Around

The sting that remains
from love's salted grains;
the ropes and the reigns,
wrapped all around you.

Like a dog that just pulled up lame
in the back of your brain,
down, down the drain,
goes the naked death of pain.
For when everybody is near,
then everywhere there is fear
of the naked death of pain.

You have to take the smoke in slow,
and let yourself go.
Love can cure your problem,
if you even have one, baby.

The red robin sings
to the bishops and the kings.
You can give your head up now,
if you even have one, baby.

The days never last,
just visions of the past.
So forget about the future,
if you even have one, baby.

I could just run away,
and never see you again,
but then…..what would that make me?
A wandering fool looking for a duel
with sleep and dream?

The serpent feeds upon
a nervous reaction,
a tiny infraction
you cannot partake in.
She said, how would you like
to die tonight?
I said, I don't really care,
without a hint of fright.

Insidious heart,
won't you leave us alone?
We do not need you anymore.
My bullets are tipped
with aphrodisiacs,
you know that it is true.
I will shoot you down,
and you will still
make sweet love to me.

You know I will fire my guns
six and one half times for you.
Everybody pray for your gods
to come down
and take you away.
I was born yesterday,
turned around once
and it was time to die.
What is the use of trying anyway,
when you only live just for the day?

Every time I look down,
I see another drowning man
with a message tied around his neck,
'It has all been such a waste.'

I know that life ridicules,
and there is no way to make it change.
So every time I see that sign,
I shake my head in haste.

Maybe someday
I won't have to beg or borrow,
but until then,
I will continue to hate tomorrow.

And who knows
where all this will lead?
The wise man always knows
when it is time to concede.
When men and women
lie with each other
laden hearts begin to destroy,
and then the mind
poignantly begins to bleed.

Comet of Love

I am driving down the highway,
you know the one I am talking about.
The overcrowded one......
people everywhere;
mind's filled with despair.
You had better get off
at the next exit,
you do not belong with me.
You are much too free.
Fly comet fly......
in circular momentum;
disparate in death,
burn your life away.
Speed time,
night light,
not just another little meteor.
Penetrate and burn
foreign surfaces.
Remember the disintegrating god,
head figure,
intrinsic body organ(ism)
for love.
Filtering a
natural presence
as infinitum,
alias-love.
Multi-wavelength,
multi-nuclear euphoria,
signifying nothing.
Painted recreation,
a woman/self defense;
Van Allen belt,
a tomb.

Keep the Change

Another island of
floating, false knowledge
made of glass,
sash, and fabric.

Ten dollars
and fifty-six cents
in change
on an empty desk
makes a
paradigm of cupidity.

Unravel the blue kelp
for the Neptune King;
the inter-societal savior,
and the soft voice
of certainty.

A super zealous
guide-leader
in pursuit of real sleep,
in scientific terms.

Watching You

The texture
of your rosy lips;
strobe light,
lava flow,
pearl eruption.
Content on
the task at hand
with little to no
disruption.

I am taken
by the passion
in the way you
stroke my mind.
I leave
the doldrums
behind,
as I find myself
in revelry,
while I watch you
make me
rise and fall
with each
new and lasting
memory.

Farewell

Ceremonial madness and the frequenting of a dream;
another lock and key for a beating heart, agleam.

Yes.

I could
f
a
l
l
for you.

Emotionally distressed
in a poetic nightmare.
Fly with me, if you can,
through the down pour;
the wind and the rain.
I need to know now,
before I cut strings.
Oh, how love brings
us climactic promise.

Ceremonial madness in a happenstance flight,
to a world far off with not a human in sight.
Perhaps, just tired and tangled with twine,
but darling I want you, I want you to be mine.
Someday lady when the moon begins to flee,
I won't look back; I will consider destiny,
I will turn around ever so quietly,
and be happy that I had you for a while.

Farewell perpetrator of mistreatment,
from a homicidal maniac.

Dark Horse

No one can ever be like me,
wanting to die
so hideously.

Oh, not another Thanatos King.
I'd give it a rest
but that is all I can sing.

Glory sweet angel, heaven's child;
you are coveting,
it is the call of the wild.

X, Y, Z, eight, nine, ten;
barter your soul
and be free again.

Good to be honest, good to be true;
and off with the old
before on with the new.

For love, love, love, makes the world go around;
it has never been lost,
it has never been found.

You'd like to meet the poet who sighed;
he is Dr. Jekyll,
and he's Mr. Hyde.

A little sunshine for a little rain;
nothing to lose,
but nothing to gain.

Unseen tomorrows, yesterday's dreams;
forgetting the present,
oh so it seems.

A love that is gone, a love that is past;
a love that is doomed
never to last.

Dark horse run, run, and run;
follow the sky
into delirium.

86 Billion Neurons Why

I know what I have to do,
but still somehow I refuse
to listen to myself.
The battle lines form
at the posterior cingulate cortex
and medial temporal lobes,
I guess that I am just madman.
I don't know why,
86 billion neurons why?
I am not enjoying life, not one tiny bit.
I feel stoned, I feel owned,
somewhere in the frontal lobe;
what a meager existence.
How sad is that?
Yet somehow I retain
enough self respect to keep
from putting a bullet
through my medulla oblongata.
How sad is that?

I don't blame anybody or everybody
for my disheartening.
I don't even blame myself
for actions long past.
None the less, none the less,
I did not ask to process
thought the way I do.
Wernicke's area and Broca's area
fight for the responsibility.
I have met the great failure,
failure in the pursuit of happiness.
Try, try, and try again.
Why bother, what is happiness anyway?
Perchance to dream?
To dream a great dream?

To conquer your expectations?
Is life merely a simple battle
of synaptic firing rates,
an ongoing war
with our own expectations?
No, life is just a tease,
to make you think
something is there
when actually, it is not.
Life is but a comparative lie,
overflowing the gutters
clogged with yesterday's leaves,
forever lost,
glossed over and evaporating
somewhere in the hippocampus.

I hope that there is no distance
in the world around the bend.
Yet possibly,
after some time spent there,
I will wish to return with help
from the basal ganglia.
Perhaps madness uprising
is all that I am;
I want you, I want you,
with my amygdala.
Maybe there is some goodness in it.
How sad is that?
How sad is our existence?
The storm is rising,
midnight has turned to disaster.
Do not blame me,
the firing is getting faster,
faster, faster, faster, and faster.
I think I feel your thalamus twitching.

The Keys Don't Tap the Same Anymore

It is all right, I tell you,
to look from behind
with one eye closed
and one in the gutter.
It is all right, I tell you,
if they, or he, or she,
tell you of your insanity;
in a low-toned mutter.

She was an angel
until I took her wings;
I left her forever,
wandering ceaselessly.
I thought that she could
find her way back home,
but life doesn't seem
to play out so easily.

Stay on the path
and don't go astray,
if you care to make it
through the next day.
Sometimes I fall asleep
wondering if I'll see tomorrow.
Sometimes it is all right, you know,
to reread "Infant Sorrow".

Sometimes you have to
bury yourself in the mud,
so you can get the jungle fever
just before the flood.
Take old man psycho,
and think of his head
smashing against a typewriter,
just before he is dead.

I have been through a dogged war,
I have been through a dogged fight;
and now you want to hassle me?
Go, and get out of my sight!

I wandered through the neighbor's castle,
I wandered through her garden home;
and now you want to bargain me?
Go, and leave me alone!

Woke up from yet another nightmare,
woke up from yet another dream;
and now you want to harbor me?
Go, and sail downstream!

My heart does not beat the same anymore,
it takes more effort, much more than before.
I think my heart is turning to coal,
ever since you torched me to the soul.

Seagull Girl

A voluptuous seagull girl
flying into turbulence,
never knowing the difference
between effort and circumstance.
A parasitic concept
that no one understands.
Holes in your ceiling
and broken rubber bands;
the rape of the mind
that comes from the glands,
a bullet proof vest,
and a nation for which it stands.

If you could just take it
for what it once was;
you could bet your life,
you know She does.
Is it you, that beauty
who needs the beast?
Is it you, who believes
in the lives deceased.
Are you there,
bored to tears, half in half?
Are you there,
my green-eyed blonde, there for a laugh?

Could it be me, totally sincere?
Could it be me, somewhere out here?
Venturous soul, so sexy and lean;
venturous soul, somewhere in between.
A light-year away, or who knows when;
a light-year away, heartbroken again.
But you knew that a great fall was in store,
with one foot out through the in door.

You keep on fighting, go out in a blaze;
perpetuating glory lost in a daze
In life's busy circle track race,
frolicking has no simple place.
It was you I could not attain,
and inside it's harder and harder to refrain.
So atop a mountain, I will climb,
but for no reason, but for no rhyme;
and giving one last intricate gasp,
I shrug off the bite of the angry asp.

Wheeled and Dealed

How come the educable majority
succumb to the ways of tomorrow?
Looking into the mirror,
I saw from one side to the other
hoping there will never be another
who will take you for your time.
Though I cannot blame you
for the shadows of yesteryear,
I will sing a tune of sorrow
hoping that you will hear
that true love locks horns with fear,
as long as I want you to be mine.

I know that you don't care,
we've reached the end of the line.
It doesn't bother me,
I've learned to accept the blue
of living in Neptune the way I do.
When I close my eyes to rest,
the paper starts to roll
underneath my eyelids;
fuel for the troll.

Someone has to dream,
someone has to scheme
another love gone awry
with nothing to redeem.
If you find yourself
playing at the Elysian Fields
where prosperity lies
protected by shields;
perhaps dismissed
by a fate that's been sealed,
or dredged up by a soul
that's been wheeled and dealed.

And if I ask a question,
I don't expect an answer to be returned.
Not that I don't care,
it is just something I've learned
from living in a society
of wise men and fools,
that send you out with blinders
to play by their rules.

But darling, I cannot do it all the time.
So, when you come down from your high,
don't be so damn serious.
If you clutter up your mind
you will make yourself delirious.
It does not matter if you live in happiness,
or if you live in sorrow;
and it does not matter where you've been,
just where you'll be tomorrow.
And I don't really care if you choose to lead,
or if you choose to follow,
as long as you'll always be mine.

If I Find My Girl

If I find my girl in the big, big city,
gonna take her home,
to comfort me.

If I find my girl in the countryside,
gonna take her in the barn,
for a hayride.

If I find my girl in the mountains, high,
gonna keep her up,
where we can fly.

If I find my girl in the rising sun,
gonna keep it hot,
and have some fun.

If I find my girl in the stars above,
gonna keep it shining,
in the house of love.

If I can't find my girl anywhere,
what's the use in living,
why should I care?

I'll take a gun from off the shelf,
pull the trigger,
and kill myself.

Butterfly Servants

What a dolorous existence;
happenstance boredom
marked in quatrain.
Flopping on the ground,
fresh out of the sound;
a message somewhat arcane.
Enemy eagles fly by candle light
hoping to latch their claws
onto something inanimate.
Uptown the celebration of
immoral acts begin.
The gutter slime society
is picketing outside,
one sign written in blood reads:

"Don't send assholes into space
to represent the human race!"

Another one reads:

"Don't let your children
grow up to be assholes!"

Butterfly servants,
that's all we are;
driving in a multi-million dollar,
frog-skin car.
Look, look, over there!
It is Ms. Ambrosia,
receptionist of the year.
The honey crowd
swarms over for autographs,
or just a glimpse
of what they cannot have.

A couple, painting yellow lines,
working the middle of the road.

Man: I wish I could get in there.
Woman: I hear the trophies get bigger every year.
Man: I wish you could get in there.
Woman: How sweet of you, my dear.

Oh well, let's just sit over here
on the curb for a while and see what happens.
Don't fall asleep though,
I think a steamroller is coming by shortly.
I don't see why the GSS is here today,
I guess they have nothing better to do.

The caterpillar wants to fly,
the risk is always there
facing the unknown.
12:35,
I am still alive.
I think I will go to bed;
hopefully, I wake up dead.

I am not quite the same as I used to be
looking through the mirror,
someone is staring at me.
His idol laughs, and turns away.
When nothing is left, you have to pray,
pray and pray,
pray all day.
Tomorrow is here to stay,
it is our day......
love child.
You should not be afraid,
the doorman has been paid.
It is our day.....
love child.
Run the water very softly,
fill my heart with pools of pain.

I will bring you flowers,
we will sing for hours;
standing in the rain.

Look at me, look at me,
a mobile magic lantern in the night.
Look at me, look at me,
shining so bright, shining so bright.

Coast to coast,
the ever most
ideals of rationality.
But rub me here,
rub me there;
smoke filled room......
of calamity.

Oh electric sky
set me free, set me free;
cast unto me
your harmony.
Change the way I think
forever......
oh butterfly,
remember me.
Remember me.

The Tale of Johnny Ice

They killed me in a snowstorm
outside the Northwest Territories,
made me out to be a legend,
but don't believe all the stories.
If you are running from something,
then you certainly are one
who made it through this life,
with much of life undone.
I married a noble princess
without any consent.
Isn't it mysterious,
the things that make us repent,
like twenty dollars
and a cold place to hide.
I have never touched a weapon,
but by weapon, I died.
If you ever find some,
you should use it while you can.
Another narcotic high
shining bright in the pan.
No one who knows you, is your friend.
Trust only, only if you dare.
Lend a helping hand to your wonder,
and be left, digging for air.
They buried me in forgotten valley
in the summer that set me free.
Remember that remembrance is mortal,
gold will wither away, just like me.

Think No. 236369

The future
you tell me
is uncertain.
Although......
I know
what I can see.
A long,
and slow
process
that moulds
this uncertain
certainty.

The First Star I See

Oh, what is the matter girl,
is it not so easy to pretend;
when the white nights have you cornered
and your innocence is near the end?
Every mountain turns to rubble
and crumbles to the sea, eventually;
just like every Romeo and Juliet
making love, passionately.
Do not fret little girl,
'tis no reason to hide,
and it wouldn't be the first time
the unknown poet lied.

But then again, perhaps,
what he speaks is somewhat true.
If that is the case, girl,
you know exactly what to do.
Just keep on, keeping on,
love life however you so please.
Don't listen to the teachers, the preachers,
or the thoughts of a self-proclaimed Sophocles'.
Play around while you can
self satisfaction is all you need.
I would like to see you later
and play for a while, if you heed.

A poet and his word are inseparable.
A dog named crucifix at my side begins to kneel
as I lay in the alley passed out from consumption,
with puncture wounds that will never heal.
Another valiant effort with no end game,
there is no reward so intense, as felicity.
No vision of hell can make me sympathize.
Will you sacrifice yourself just a little bit for me?

You might mask yourself in the process,
a pathetic ritual but who would ever know?
It might help control your inhibitions,
let down your hair girl, let it flow.
Is anyone out there listening to what I'm saying,
wondering what the fuck is going in here?
The dissatisfied always end up praying
for all of their ills and wills, to disappear.
Two burnt souls posing with gun at head,
in front of misconception's waving flag.
Together we will learn to break all the rules
before we wind up in the same body bag.

Maybe I'll find some gold before the storm hits,
a dwelling disfigurement in my mind.
Maybe I'll just stand here in the freezing rain,
another day of treatment so unkind.
In this day and age, that is finding a loophole,
weave your way in-between and fill a gap.
Don't give me any heartache about your morals,
I've had it up to here with all that crap.
Steer clear of my love, the apple is poison,
you can tell the stars apart from here.
Sometimes you're jealous of another fantasy,
but each one is another distant light-year.

I would share all of mine with you,
if you would agree to share all of yours
I never got to go to sleep when I was so tired;
remember when it rains, it always pours.
I think I am coming to the end of a procession.
Lesson number one: there is little time to breathe.
You can figure out the rest on your own time;
if you forget how to smile, you can seethe.

Angel Scream

If I get my hands on a loaded gun,
gonna take chance and fly to the sun.
If I get my hands on a cyanide pill,
gonna meet you at the top of the hill.

If I get my hands on a sharpened knife,
gonna take a chance and end my life.
But before I drift into the lonely dream,
I want to hear my angel scream

If I find myself in the driver's seat,
gonna take us down a dead end street.
If I find myself up on nineteenth floor,
gonna take a leap to nevermore.

If I find myself in an ocean deep,
gonna sink into the endless sleep.
But before I float down the eternal stream,
I want to hear my angel scream

If I find myself with a razor sharp,
gonna slit my wrists and play the harp.
If I find myself by a fire station,
gonna toss the match, self-incineration.

If I find myself on a bridge so high,
gonna look at you and wave goodbye.
But before my eyes give a final gleam,
I want to hear my angel scream.

Truth's Yield

Is it just a memory?
I only find it slips
away
from me.
The nighttime
brings me pain.

Masquerade,
masquerade,
hidden reflections
of an escapade.
Locked onto sadness,
locked onto scheme,
focus of attention
to the dream.
See yourself on
a charcoal horse,
singing a song
in the code of Morse.

Everybody wants to die
it is just a matter of when,
not why.
White rain falls freely
in the yellow field.
Blue baskets fill
with the constancies
of truth's yield.

Spotlight Love

Is this true,
can it really be;
a starlight princess
next to me?

Her hair so soft,
her smile so bright;
her eyes do glisten
with endless delight.

Oh, starlight princess!
Oh, starlight princess!

I like the way
you shine on me;
everything you do
brings me ecstasy.

I am floating away
on the clouds of a new day;
a poet on the run,
when I'm closer to the sun.

Painted Desert

This lock and chain
I hold in my hand
is just for you, as I planned.
I was thinking about that day,
a long time ago,
when I found it in
Painted Desert land.
The key was missing,
I've been searching ever since;
don't try to convince......me, otherwise.
Don't you even......try.
Up in the mountains, across the plateau,
In the dark, and light of the moon.
I know I'll find it, someday soon.
I know, I know that I can.

Another sufficient
picture of reality,
building sections of sanctity.
Send me turbulence,
I'll send you need;
spiritual exercise,
labyrinthine universe,
I will be your lead.
Do not heed......
speed, speed,
speed on past the doom.
Ten thousand objects
within the void;
follow the blood on the tracks,
take us back to the age of wax.
Something I never thought I'd see,
disappearing in the wind.

Over Your Shoulder

Pick up the pieces that make a rainbow,
lying in the corner amidst a pile of hearts,
I see a clock that has stopped;
broken time is always free.
What is the use of hanging around
to be what you really want to be?
I will take a few pills for the rest of my life,
run to the door, nothing is out there anymore.

The future is futile, an embryonic magma;
a little flow, then a period of hardening.
Counting my coins on a Sunday afternoon,
man should not live on bread alone.
Take me to a place where I can run free.
I am waiting for a special hating to occur.
Unless I am mistaking, you are falling
out of love with her.

We come from triton,
our father is your father.
We come for death.

You look around for friends and frowns,
but all you see are smiling faces.
I am living in the town where I was born,
but I've never felt so far from home.
I am waiting for a special hating to occur.
Unless I am mistaking, you are falling
out of love with her
and I, I want to take over.

Two souls forever bound,
together, by an ancient dream;
lost on the endeavor, waiting for a fatal scream,
and I, I will take over.

If you don't believe
and you can't conceive,
then I, I will take over.

Look into the room,
see everyone in disguise.
But it is so hard to notice
with blood in your eyes.
If you have no fear, you're not afraid to ask why.
If you have no fear, you're not afraid to die.

So, tell me a story of hatred,
busted dreams and worn out hopes.
Don't tell me the fight is over
when you're hung up on the ropes.
Your heart may be stopped,
but you don't know the meaning of life and death.
There is so little in between,
between each and every breath.
Gods all around running for air,
doesn't really matter, no need to care.
It is a paper thin day, only if you let it,
and a hacksaw day, only if you regret it.

So, look around the room,
see everyone in disguise.
It is so damn hard to see,
with blood in your eyes.
The next time you are losing,
not even in the game.
Look over your shoulder,
I'll tell you who's to blame.

Poetic Slur

I'd like to roll my hands
up and down, across your breasts.
Don't take it wrong, babe,
it is just a poetic slur.
If I had a thought on my mind,
and I thought it was good;
I'd tell you I love you
and you know that I would.

Hey Romeo, you didn't understand;
nobody cares about you, man.
That is what you get
for a love that's been paid;
emotionless passion
in a bed that is never made.

Confused Lady

I am glad that you did ask,
but I can never remove this mask.
I am afraid to unravel
all the places I'd like to travel......with you.
I cannot release my last little piece......of mind.
Oh, life has been so unkind to me.

Beautiful confused lady, come sit by my side;
share yourself with me,
I need a place to hide......my feelings.
I'd like to spend the evening with you,
doing the things you love to do.

It is the confusion that I see,
that makes you so attractive to me.
I could sit here and sing all day,
but you don't listen, so I am going away
without you......far away without you.

Beautiful confused lady,
hand me your heart.
You feel so abandoned,
I won't tear it apart.
Let us watch the sun ascending
while naively pretending
that love lasts forever,
and ever, and ever.

I could sit here and sing all night,
but you don't listen, so I'll take the next flight
without you......far away without you.

Shadows Under the Rainbow

There are many things in life I can do without
but without you, I'd forever drift about
beneath the lonely lover's rainbow;
with no one to talk to, no one to know.
Nowhere to go. Nowhere to go.
For this is where stricken hearts do stroll
waiting for misery to take its toll.
You are the one I cannot resist
when my ship is sinking into the abyss
you are always there, there to assist;
to reach way down and pull me out
if I refuse to come, you insist.
So when my life is like rain
and the wind doesn't blow;
when I've got no one to talk to
and nowhere to go
I look for you......
my girl with the glow.
For it is your sunshine
that makes my heart grow.
And whenever I am near you,
I must let you know
or it is back to the rain,
the misery, and the woe.

Once again I need you;
please help me out of the abyss,
and this time as you lift me up
I will tell you this.
I love you, I love you,
more than anyone could ever know.
I love you, I love you,
although it doesn't always show.
I love you, I love you,
please hold on and never let go.

You might have thought I didn't love you,
but you have never been so wrong.
Ever since the day we've met,
we've never been apart so long.
I am starting to believe you don't really mind,
that is why I am writing this song;
with hope that someday soon we'll be back again
forever side by side, where we belong.
Sunny days, they last forever
when you are walking at my side,
always knowing that you were thinking,
someday I will be his lovely bride.
But now I am not sure if you even care,
or still feel anything inside;
so I am crying out to you,
no longer can I let my feelings hide.

I remember good times, how much we loved
and always let each other know.
Whatever one did and wherever one went,
the other was sure to follow.
But now I am not sure if you feel the same,
or will feel the same tomorrow;
it hurts so bad that I must cry out
as I sit here in pain and sorrow.
Please let me know that you still love me
and always let me know,
for there is no place in this world
that without you I would go.
And I promise that I will do the same
to always reassure,
that my love for you is infinite
and forever pure.

I send you one last message as tears roll down my face;
without your loving touch my life has no place.
So again I tell you, as I wipe another tear from my eye;
without your loving touch I will just wither away and die.

My Senses are Being Stripped

Don't bother writing a letter in return;
I don't see too well, you know.
Don't even bother calling me;
because my hearing was next to go.

You see the only way to heal
my dying love......is to feel......so
Come and make me feel.
I need to......feel.

To smell......the fragrance of your skin;
To touch......the beauty of your face;
To taste......the passion of your kiss;
I need to......feel.

Come make me feel,
if you can find the time.
And with what you did last weekend,
there is no reason or rhyme;
and what are you doing this weekend,
that you cannot find the time?

If you do not respond soon,
I'll take it in my heart;
that time is life,
and life is change;
time to make a new start.

For if the next sense goes,
then it is three of five;
and no longer can love
remain......alive!

From a Poet's Vantage Point

Sitting here
atop sanctity hill,
I look up
but can only see down,
down the endless street
of gothic gloom.

The bride dresses
in a long black gown,
strolling down the aisle
she meets her groom,
who looks at her
with a long black frown.

Designed Fate

From Oldowan tools
to flying machines,
we teach our children
how to think;
but only by our means
......of desolation,
our ideals of grandeur,
and our premonition
of designed fate.
Insistence
is what makes me
so irate.

When an hour ends,
how much time
has really passed?
Of all the replies I know,
sixty minutes is the last;
for it is the fool
who plays these
number games.

Do not believe
all that is said,
or these number games
will leave you for dead.
After all,
who thinks of growing old?
Certainly those
that do as they are told.

Who is the Artist

You are the artist......not me;
without you, my symbols are mere poetry.
You are the artist......not me;
it is not my words, but what in them, you see.
You are the artist......not me;
I am just wanting to be free.
You are the artist......not me;
now quietly close our mind and let us be.
You are the artist......not me.

The Gondolier

Oh, how I wish that I could leave
this gallery of derision
behind.
Inside the gallery are
the dungeons of despair.
The dungeons of despair, babe,
the dungeons of despair;
where everybody lives together
pretending they are weak and blind.
And you want to know,
why I've lost my mind.
You want to
be
in
love,
and
me
in
love;
be out of love and be a poet.
How many more times must I miss
the boat ride off this land
of wear and tear.
How often are we unaware
when love is all there is to share?
Because in the end, we realize
what was made between the thighs.
Plunder to know,
wonder to show
how much love you make or take.
Live inside the hearts you break.
So,
pound the stake, pound it good.
Pound the stake as you should,
then shine your grin and walk away.

The message from the gondolier
is all so illusive and all so clear;
guaranteed to make your heart steer
off the beaten path of love, in fear.
Fear of love, fear of life
filled with loneliness and strife.
Waiting for dreamboats on the horizon
to disappear as we wisen
up.
The violin plays a melody
for you to sit and ponder.
Does absence make the heart grow fonder,
or fonder of hate, when love goes yonder?
Close your eyes, begin to wander.
Wonder whether or not you're alive,
and as you wonder, remember
all the times you woke up in her bed
arms wrapped around, wishing you were dead.
Like I said,
does absence make the heart grow fonder?
Everybody asks the question
at some point in their life.
Every melody sounds like a sad, sad song
when you are floating on misery's waters.
Sometimes you just have to know
which way the wind shall blow
so......
so you stick your head up and breathe
for a while, a little while.
While I am unabashedly instigating;
causing turmoil and oppression,
waiting for no response.
Message from the gondolier,
enjoy the pain;
it is what keeps us sane.

Another Day

The farther one travels,
the less one travels.

Just a god;
justification of the mind,
and prevention
of psychic immobility

What makes you feel safe?
a fantasy comes in
from out of the rain.

A day that I cannot recall,
is no day at all.

There are so many days
that I lived
with you,
they pass through the alleys
in my mind.

They never go away,
a day......is a day
when
I am with you.

The Stainless Steel Vault

I vanished inside
a stainless steel vault.
All of my dreams
have come to a halt.

Pictures of Eden
flash through my head,
reminding me of
the time I was dead.

I met a far away girl
on a baby grand,
and said this is your spirit
right here in my hand.

This is your spirit,
play it slow.
Before you know it
the turbulent flow

will overcome you
and leave you choking.
A poet's talent,
thought provoking.

Wet

I've been thinking about ceremony,
I've been thinking about blood;
I've been thinking about the calm
before the flood.

I've been thinking about life,
I've been thinking about lust;
I've been thinking about the girl
known as angel dust.

I've been thinking about sensation,
I've been thinking about pain;
I've been thinking about pandemonium
in the back of my brain.

I've been thinking about distortion,
I've been thinking about pain;
I've been thinking about the journey
through love's terrain.

I've been thinking about psychosis,
I've been thinking about pain;
I've been thinking about my life
on a tangent plane.

I've been thinking about poetry,
I've been thinking about death;
I've been thinking about the smoke
coming out of my breath.

Miss America

I am con-fused again,
where can you be......
my Miss America
(girl with the golden tan)?
The sun is gone,
'tis difficult to see......
the world turning.

I am con-fused again,
where can you be......
my Miss America
(girl without a man)?
The sun is gone,
'tis difficult to see......
the world adjourning.

I am con-fused again,
where can you be......
my Miss America
(girl without a plan)?
The sun is gone,
'tis difficult to see......
the world burning.

Oracle of the Cephalopod

An enigmatic life form
of people who disapprove.
Ode to the eternal enemies
lying in the big city;
two societies and two women,
not to prosperous.
Who holds the key
to our own identities?
With vengeance on its mind,
what is the shadow within
its own environment?
Everyone seems a bit dissatisfied
when they learn of their learning.
One can always choose
between learning
and the way they want to learn.
Make your own adventure
a masterpiece.

Myths and misconceptions
of body chemistry;
it is not in what you have,
but in how you put these
pieces together.
Death results in
tantalizing mysteries.
No one likes the real you
(the blackened refried you),
because they are afraid
that you'll undo
their hypocrisies.
An unchained man
will terrorize the populace;
chase down their dreams
and bite them off at the neck.

How many people out there
know how I feel
(tentacles grab you)?
I am sure there are many,
but we will never
have the opportunity
to gravitate together
(metaphysically speaking),
if you know what I mean.

Life is just a three-ring circus
of ups and downs;
such a brilliant creator,
but insomniacs never dream.
Leaving unknowledgeable sleepers
some advice,
'don't dream of tomorrow'.
Things do change
I found Aladdin's lamp,
but I turned down the wishes.
I just don't care,
there is nothing worth wishing for.
A celebration of life,
the controversial nature
of a cephalopod's mind.
We are just two intelligent creatures
plotting to overthrow
the universe.

Leeway

Is it not peculiar,
how everyone turns out
and burns out
just like the rest
because they think
it a necessary will?
Look at all the children
glistening, listening
to Mother Goose
and reading Dr. Seuss,
forever after.
But then, but then,
oh when, oh when,
the nimbus comes around.
The light makes sound
and you cease the laughter.
Mapping out the brain,
mapping out the ocean,
mapping out the pain,
mapping out the stars,
searching for a master.
Painting a large black hole,
a silhouetted vision
of what salvation is
meant to be;
a leeway to
a most valid thought,
that I ought not to be
an orgasmic continuity
of scattered processes.

Hell's Hundred Hectares

Some souls are darkened,
violently walking
in the midst of normalcy.
In the prison of mediocrity,
everyone talking;
all I here is
"Baa baa baa!"
Suddenly a club
takes down an innocent
element;
a common grain of sand
never to be missed.

The Temptuous Temptress Empress

Willow of the winds,
you contemplate in dream,
the resurrection of a time
somewhere in between
the fiery distant future
and the icy frozen past;
upon the starry-eyed
your sultry spell is cast.
Melting rocks in silence;
a lost and languid liquid glow.
Here she comes again,
tumultuous thoughts begin to flow.

Blending the lighter side of sadness
with the brighter side of madness.
Adding a little bit of somber tone
and mixing in some parts unknown.
The brewing up of miser
in its purest form;
leaves us in the midst
of her everyday storm.

Unorganized acts of consciousness
placate the heartless anonymity
of a mistaken dream sequence,
and all of its calamity.
Somewhere we live our worst nightmare
and somewhere, in a paradise we dwell.
For the world has infinite endings,
and beginnings......infinite as well.
However, let us never forget
the world has an infinite number of nows;
look into the eyes of the Tempest Empress
and repeat to her your vows:

The space between now
and loving you for the first time
is eternally vacant and vast.
Lost eyes, shapely thighs,
and ruby lips forever gleaming;
screaming at the past.

She is not for the weak,
not for the weary,
and not for the faint-hearted.
Never dream too softly
for life has a way of ending
before it has ever started.

The Kangaroo

Everybody knew
like the kangaroo, who
locked up inside to stew, who
bouncing in my head
on and off of the wall
while stammering down the hall.
The overlong sleeves help to restrain
the asylum from the insane, who
deemed me to be inane
like the kangaroo, who
locked up inside of them too,
never having to contend
they lack the ability to comprehend
a non-ideological system of thought.

I know what you think
another one on the brink
just like the kangaroo, who
lives inside of you.

Misery Loves Calligraphy

Misery loves calligraphy,
and typology,
and a blackwing pencil
jammed in the side
of your neck.

A speck of hope
on the backspace key;
strikeout the last dream
and rewrite the fate.
Mine is yours,
and yours to hate.

The world begins
to masturbate,
and all that is left
is a bunch of letters
floating at random.

```
 D   Gj.m  s
So  v    Ir cj
    H  Eo   A  W
 h    O  Wi  db
 b   n   H   j
 .
```

Isms

Keep your art to yourself,
Roscoe P. Tanner.
The world revolves around
corporate idealism
not your stupid poetry.

The idiot savants
gifted in making deals
are the reason life goes on.

Yeah, yeah, yeah
Corporate Joe Co., Inc, Fuck-n-Fuck;

I deal 'isms'?
You deal 'isms',
We all deal 'isms'!

Thank you......self.

About the Author

Born and raised in St. Petersburg, Florida, Thomas Walker left a promising career with an international architecture firm for the adventures of Alaska. He has been living in Eagle River, Alaska ever since, and is forever afflicted with the disease so greatly known as......poetry.

Thomas Walker Publications
Eagle River, Alaska